"The mind is everything.
What you think, you become."

—Buddha

Copyright @ 2025
Corinne Coe
All rights reserved
First release: July 2025

CORINNE COE

Think Positive Feel Positive

*Change your mindset to transform yourself
and enhance your life.*

COPYRIGHT & MEDICAL DISCLAIMER

Copyright © Corinne Coe 2025

Corinne Coe has asserted her right under the Copyright, Designs and Patents Act 1988 to be recognised as the author of this book.

This publication represents a non-fiction work that is grounded in the author's personal experiences and reflections, as well as those of individuals who have preceded them. The author asserts that, aside from specific exceptions, the content of this book is accurate and true to the best of her recollection of events.

The author of this book does not dispense medical advice or prescribe the use of any technique as a form of treatment for physical, emotional, or medical problems without the advice of a physician, either directly or indirectly. The 'intent' of the author is only to offer information of a general educational nature to help you in your quest for emotional and psychological well-being. If you use any of the information in this book for yourself, which is your constitutional right, the author and publisher assume no responsibility for your actions.

All rights reserved. No part of this publication may be reproduced, stored in a retrieval system, or transmitted in any form or by any means, electronic, medical, photocopying, recording, or otherwise, without the author's prior written permission.

First published in Australia in its current form in 2025 by Corinne Coe.

Publisher's website address: www.corinnecoe.com

Cover & Typeset by Laura Antonioli

ISBN:
Paperback: 978-0-9946461-3-2
eBook: 978-0-9946461-4-9

All rights reserved, printed in Australia.

FIRST EDITION, July 2025.

Positive Thinking, Positive Feeling: *Affirmations*

1.

Before accepting a negative thought as fact, take a moment to question it. Ask yourself, "What evidence do I have for and against to support this belief?"

Before accepting a negative thought as a definitive truth, take a moment to examine it critically. Pause, breathe, and ask yourself, "What tangible evidence do I have that supports this belief?" Reflecting on the validity of your thoughts can often provide a clearer perspective. Imagine you are involved in a court case; what evidence would be accepted to support your case?

2.

Avoid making conclusions based on assumptions; base them on facts instead.

Avoid drawing conclusions based on assumptions; instead, ground your judgments in concrete facts. For instance, rather than speculating about a future event, concentrate on the solid evidence that supports its likelihood. Let your decisions be guided by what you can observe and verify, ensuring that your understanding is based on reality rather than mere conjecture.

3.

If you seldom receive criticism, it might be worth considering it as an unspoken compliment.

If you notice that criticism comes your way infrequently, it might be wise to view this lack of feedback as a subtle yet meaningful compliment. This could imply that your work or behaviour is generally well-received and appreciated, making any critique all the more significant when it does arise.

4.

Before assessing the worst-case scenario, evaluate its likelihood using the information and facts available.

Before diving into the worst-case scenario, take a moment to assess the probability of such an outcome based on the information and facts at your disposal. For instance, if your doctor reaches out to arrange an appointment to discuss test results but does not express any urgency or suggest that the situation is dire, it may be worth considering that the news might not be as unfavourable as you fear. Reflect on these nuances; a calm approach can often illuminate the situation, providing a more balanced perspective before jumping to conclusions.

5.

When concluding, it is crucial to avoid relying solely on the viewpoints of a small minority. Instead, you should place greater confidence in the beliefs and actions of the more significant majority.

When drawing conclusions, it is essential to refrain from basing your judgment solely on the opinions of a small minority group. While diverse perspectives can be valuable, they do not necessarily reflect the broader sentiment or reality of the situation. Therefore, it is advisable to place greater emphasis on the beliefs and actions of the larger majority, as they often provide a more accurate representation of the prevailing attitudes and values within a given context. By prioritizing the majority view, you can ensure that your conclusions are grounded in a more comprehensive understanding of the issues at hand.

> Self-care is not a waste of time. Self-care makes your use of time more sustainable.
>
> Jackie Viramontez

6.

*Don't blame yourself for
things outside your control.*

There's no reason to blame yourself for circumstances beyond your control. Take, for instance, a situation where a project failed to meet its deadline; if that happened due to external factors, such as unexpected changes in regulations, resource shortages, or unanticipated delays from the supplier, it's essential to recognise that these were not issues caused by your actions. Allow yourself to understand that sometimes, despite our best efforts, outcomes are influenced by external factors.

7.

Pay attention to what most people say and how they behave; you'll often notice they engage in the same actions that you fear will draw their judgment.

Take a moment to observe the behaviours and expressions of those around you; you might discover that many people display reactions similar to your own anxieties about being judged. We all experience moments of embarrassment or regret, but the key difference lies in how we respond to these situations. By choosing to laugh at our mistakes instead of dwelling on them, we can feel more at ease in social situations. Additionally, when you shift your focus from yourself to others, you'll begin to realise that everyone faces similar challenges. This realisation can foster a deeper sense of connection and provide comfort, reminding you that you are not alone during tough times.

8.

Avoid setting yourself up for failure; instead, establish realistic expectations.

Avoid placing yourself in a situation where failure could occur by setting expectations that are grounded in reality. For example, if the average person typically requires a certain amount of time to complete a specific task, it's unwise to expect yourself to finish significantly faster or slower than that benchmark. Instead, strive to establish your standards and goals based on what most people can realistically achieve, allowing for a more balanced and achievable approach to your pursuits.

9.

Don't be afraid to fail at new things; some skills, systems, or knowledge require time and experience to master.

Embrace the idea that failure is a natural part of trying new things; mastering various skills, processes, or areas of knowledge demands not only time but also the insights gained from experience. Don't shy away from the challenges that come with learning something new, as each setback presents an opportunity for growth and improvement on your path to proficiency.

10.

Don't confuse capacity and capability.

It's essential to differentiate between capacity and capability. Capability refers to your skills and competencies—your ability to perform specific tasks or effectively fulfil your job responsibilities. On the other hand, capacity involves the actual availability or readiness to execute those skills, which can be influenced by various factors, such as physical or mental health. For example, even if you possess the necessary expertise to excel in your role, an injury could limit your capacity to perform at your best, making it challenging to carry out your job effectively despite your qualifications and experience.

> Balance between work and pleasure, giving and receiving, seriousness and levity, creates a happy and healthy life.
>
> Kathy Freston

11.

If you can't do something that someone else can, remember that what they see as a strength might be your weakness, and vice versa.

When you find yourself struggling with something that someone else seems to handle effortlessly, it's essential to remember that their strengths might highlight your own areas for improvement, and the same can apply in reverse. Take a moment to reflect: while they may excel in organisation, displaying a natural knack for keeping things in order and following structured plans, you might possess vibrant creativity that allows you to think outside the box and come up with innovative ideas. Embracing this perspective can help you appreciate the unique talents each person contributes, fostering a sense of mutual respect and collaboration.

12.

Whenever you catch yourself overthinking, consider how many times you've done it before and whether what you were overthinking actually happened.

Whenever you find yourself caught in a cycle of overthinking, take a moment to reflect on your past experiences. Consider how often you've let your mind spiral into worry and doubt. Then, think about the specific situations that occupied your thoughts—how many of them actually came to fruition? By recalling these instances, you might realise that many of your concerns never materialised, which can help you regain perspective and calm your mind.

13.

*Before accepting criticism,
make sure it is constructive rather
than destructive.*

If you find yourself facing frequent criticism about a specific aspect of your behaviour or work, it may be beneficial to view it as constructive feedback. Constructive criticism is usually offered with the intention of promoting your growth and improvement, often arising from its impact on the critic's experience or feelings. Conversely, if the criticism is infrequent or feels unjustified, it may stem from a more destructive intent. In such instances, it's crucial to critically assess the motives behind the feedback, as it might be a form of manipulation, an attempt to exert control, or even a subtle putdown intended to undermine your confidence. Recognising the distinction between these types of criticism can be instrumental in navigating personal development and maintaining a healthy self-image.

14.

The next time you find yourself worrying about a stressful situation, remind yourself of the many occasions you've faced, managed, and overcome challenges by relying on your coping skills.

When you start to feel anxious about a challenging situation, take a moment to pause and reflect on the tough moments you've faced in the past. Allow this reflection to reassure you that you have the tools to handle whatever comes your way. Trust in your ability to manage difficult situations. Think back to the many times you confronted challenges head-on and emerged stronger by using your coping mechanisms and problem-solving skills. Consider the resilience you've demonstrated, drawing on your inner resources to navigate adversity and find solutions when obstacles seemed insurmountable.

15.

Worrying is a natural response that can lead you to solutions. A certain amount of worry is necessary, as it triggers adrenaline and boosts your motivation to tackle problems.

Worrying is a common emotional response that can act as a valuable signal, encouraging you to find solutions to your challenges. This instinctive reaction activates your body's adrenaline response, sharpening your focus and energising your motivation, propelling you to face problems directly. Thus, a certain level of worry can be advantageous, serving as a catalyst for proactive thinking and actions in the quest for resolution.

> I will not let anyone walk through my mind with their dirty feet.
>
> Gandhi

16.

When you find yourself worrying about something, take a moment to assess just how serious the issue really is and respond accordingly. The seriousness depends on the potential consequences or impact the problem may have on you or your life.

When you notice yourself spiralling into worry over a particular issue, it's important to pause and assess the true significance of the matter at hand. Consider evaluating the potential consequences or the overall impact that the problem might have on your life. For instance, if you find yourself grappling with a challenge that you would rate as a mere 2 out of 10 in severity, it's crucial to allow your emotional response to align accordingly. Instead of reacting with an intensity that corresponds to an 8 out of 10, which would likely amplify your stress unnecessarily, aim to keep your concerns in perspective. By doing this, you can respond appropriately to the situation, preserving your emotional well-being while addressing the issue at hand.

17.

Be proactive instead of reactive. Reflect on whether you are addressing a genuine problem or simply worrying. Is the issue likely to arise, or are you just assuming it will?

Adopt a proactive mindset rather than merely reacting to situations as they arise. Take a moment to reflect and ask yourself if you are genuinely facing a real issue or if you're simply caught up in unnecessary worry. Consider the likelihood of the problem actually occurring—are your concerns grounded in realistic possibilities, or are you just making assumptions about what might happen? This self-reflection can help you distinguish between constructive problem-solving and unproductive anxiety.

18.

How many times have you assumed a problem would arise but didn't? Have you ever anticipated an issue, bracing for its impact, only to discover that it never materialised?

Have you ever found yourself preparing for a daunting challenge, mentally rehearsing how it could disrupt your life, only to realise that the anticipated event never occurred? It's an odd phenomenon how our minds often conjure scenarios that we believe are bound to happen, yet in reality, everything turns out just fine. This experience serves as a powerful reminder of the benefits of a positive mindset. When we reflect on our experiences and acknowledge that many fears are unfounded, we also come to understand that we shouldn't always trust what we assume might happen. This realisation can help us approach challenges with greater confidence and openness.

19.

Don't let the uncertainties of future events weigh on your mind, especially those that haven't yet unfolded as you picture them.

To effectively navigate uncertainties about future events, focusing on the present rather than getting caught up in hypotheticals is essential. Redirecting your energy towards current experiences can help foster a mindset that is open to new possibilities. Attempting to visualise an entire scenario with limited information can be unproductive. By concentrating on the present and honing your ability to handle any upcoming changes or challenges, just as you have already proven to yourself, you can empower yourself to move forward with confidence and clarity. This approach creates space for positive experiences and personal growth. It not only helps alleviate stress but also enhances your overall well-being.

20.

When confronted with difficult decisions, pause for a moment to consider whether you're attempting to understand the full picture while only viewing a handful of scattered pieces of the puzzle.

When faced with difficult decisions, it's helpful to take a moment to pause and reflect on your understanding of the situation. Are you focused on the bigger picture, or are you mainly viewing a few disconnected fragments? Recognising the limitations of your perspective can be invaluable in the decision-making process. Consider seeking additional information that can provide clarity. Allow yourself the time to gather the insights necessary to guide you in making a well-informed choice. Adopting this constructive approach not only fosters better outcomes but also enhances your understanding of the situation at hand.

> Taking care of myself doesn't mean 'me first'.
> It means 'me too'.
>
> L.R. Knost

21.

How often have you questioned your decisions, only to find they ended up being the best choices after all?

Have you ever found yourself questioning your decisions, wondering if you made the right choice? It's fascinating to recognise that many of those choices often lead to positive outcomes. Embracing this understanding can greatly enhance your confidence in making future decisions. Trust in your intuition and experiences, and remember that each choice is an opportunity for growth and learning.

22.

Instead of getting bogged down by the trivial challenges of everyday life, it's far more beneficial to channel your energy and emotions towards the issues that genuinely impact your life.

Consider how each minor annoyance fits into the broader context of your life. By prioritising genuine matters of importance, you can free yourself from the burden of inconsequential distractions that only serve to cloud your mind and complicate your emotions. Embrace the clarity that comes from recognising what truly matters, enabling you to invest your energy in pursuits that foster growth and fulfilment.

23.

Rocks symbolise major problems that significantly impact you, pebbles represent minor issues, and sand signifies problems that won't affect you at all. Focus on the rocks and don't waste your energy on the pebbles or sand.

Rocks represent the significant challenges in your life—those major problems that can profoundly impact your well-being and daily functioning. Pebbles, conversely, symbolise the minor inconveniences that may arise but ultimately have little influence on your overall happiness. Lastly, sand signifies the trivial issues that are inconsequential, having minimal to no effect on your life. By concentrating your energy on addressing the rocks, you can navigate your path more effectively, rather than getting bogged down by the pebbles and sand that don't truly matter.

24.

When addressing concerns, it's vital to refrain from drawing broad conclusions based on minor errors. A single mistake does not define an individual's overall abilities or character.

When addressing concerns, it's crucial to avoid jumping to sweeping conclusions based on minor slip-ups. A single, small mistake should never be seen as an indicator of a person's overall capabilities or character. Instead, it's vital to step back and consider the broader context, recognising that everyone has the potential to make odd blunders without these missteps overshadowing their true skills or approach to tasks. By maintaining this perspective, we can promote a more understanding and supportive environment that encourages growth and learning.

25.

If you often revisit or reflect on past conversations, consider whether your negative thoughts align with the other person's body language, words, or facial expressions.

Evaluate the outcomes of your interactions by closely observing the behaviours and reactions of others rather than relying on assumptions or preconceived notions. When reflecting on past conversations, take a moment to consider whether any negative thoughts you might have are supported by tangible signs from the other person, such as their body language, the tone of their voice, and the expressions on their face. Look for cues that reveal their feelings or attitudes, as these can offer valuable insights that clarify the true nature of the exchange.

> I've had a lot of worries in my life, most of which never happened.
>
> Mark Twain

26.

Worrying can't prevent events from happening. Instead, channel that energy into motivating yourself to seek solutions or alternatives that can help lessen the impact.

Constantly worrying brings no real control over the events unfolding in our lives; it merely creates a cycle of anxiety without any tangible results. Rather than letting that swirling energy of concern dominate your thoughts, consider redirecting it towards constructive action. Focus on finding solutions or exploring alternative approaches that can effectively reduce the potential consequences of those challenges. Embracing a proactive mindset empowers you and helps you discover ways to lessen the impact of possible difficulties.

27.

Minimise emotional reactions that could hinder your ability to think clearly when faced with challenges.

By practising controlled, deep, and slow breathing, you can effectively lower adrenaline levels, which often exacerbate feelings of anxiety and urgency. This deliberate focus on your breath fosters a sense of calm, allowing your mind to clear and sharpening your cognitive abilities. As you engage in these breathing techniques, envision inhaling deeply, filling your lungs completely, and exhaling slowly, releasing tension with each breath. This rhythmic pattern not only promotes relaxation but also helps distance you from the emotional turmoil that can arise during problem-solving. Embracing this tranquil mindset empowers you to think more rationally and navigate complexities with greater ease and clarity, ultimately enhancing your overall problem-solving skills.

28.

Often, it's not the circumstances themselves that create a problem, but rather how you perceive them. Gather objective facts to gain a clearer understanding and interpret matters accurately.

Often, the difficulties we face stem less from the actual circumstances we encounter and more from how we choose to interpret and understand those situations. Our perceptions can be significantly affected by our emotions, past experiences, and biases, which may lead us to misinterpret what is truly occurring. To gain a clearer and more realistic view of our challenges, it's vital to gather objective facts. This involves stepping back, analysing the situation without emotional interference, and focusing on concrete details. By doing this, we can develop a more accurate understanding of our circumstances, enabling us to address them with greater clarity and insight. This process not only helps in navigating the present more effectively but also empowers us to make informed decisions about how to respond.

29.

Recognise the significance of being adaptable when facing challenges beyond your control.

Instead of using your energy to control what lies beyond your influence, focus on nurturing a flexible mindset. Seek out innovative solutions that can significantly enhance your strategy. Adopting this perspective will empower you to tackle challenges with agility, enabling you to respond proactively to shifts in your environment. By welcoming change rather than resisting it, you can discover and seize new opportunities for personal and professional growth. Take a moment to reflect on times when you initially felt overwhelmed by change, yet ultimately managed to navigate through it. Consider whether your belief in your inability to cope made the experience more stressful, or if you truly faced challenges in managing the transition.

30.

When it comes to decision-making, don't hesitate to draw on the experiences and insights of those around you. Keep in mind that the people you consult have likely been in the same boat.

When making decisions, draw on the rich reservoir of experiences, knowledge, and skills possessed by those around you. Each person provides unique insights shaped by their individual journeys, acting as a compass for navigating choices. Don't hesitate to seek advice or perspectives from others; their contributions can illuminate paths you may not have considered before, ultimately guiding you towards more informed and thoughtful decisions.

> We all have an unsuspected reserve of strength inside that emerges when life puts us to the test.
>
> Isabel Allende

31.

Before seeking reassurance, take a moment to reflect on the feedback you've received. Was it negative? Think about whether you've achieved what you intended to accomplish.

Before seeking reassurance, pause for a moment to reflect on the feedback you've received. Assess whether the feedback was mainly negative and consider how well you've met your personal goals. Think about your past experiences: how often has your need for reassurance been justified? This introspective process can offer valuable insights into your feelings and the legitimacy of your concerns, ultimately fostering personal growth and building greater confidence in yourself.

32.

When setting goals, assess your resources, including skills, experience, and time, to ensure they are realistic and achievable. Goals ought to challenge you while remaining attainable to foster motivation and success.

When you're setting goals, it's crucial to ensure they are both realistic and achievable. Take a moment to assess whether you have the necessary resources at your disposal. Consider your skills, past experience, and knowledge relevant to the goal. It's also important to check if you have the time to devote to this effort. If you discover you lack any of these essential components, you might be setting yourself up for disappointment and failure. Remember, goals should stretch your capabilities, but they should also be achievable to foster motivation and success.

33.

Focus on outcomes instead of getting bogged down in details or chasing perfection. Striving for flawless results can cause stress and impede progress.

Reflect on whether details truly impact results. Is the content most important, or are embellishments necessary? Shift your focus towards achieving meaningful outcomes rather than getting bogged down in minutiae or striving for unattainable perfection. The relentless quest for flawless results often creates unnecessary stress and can impede your progress. Take a moment to observe those around you—how much of their lives genuinely reflects perfection? Who is there to judge their efforts? Consider whether the intricate details you fixate on will genuinely affect the final results. Is it the substance and quality of the content that matters most, or are those additional embellishments really vital to overall success?

34.

Don't stress about being judged by those who haven't taken the time to genuinely understand you or your story. People who judge often do so to cover up their insecurities and project a false sense of confidence.

Don't let the fear of judgment from those who haven't made the effort to genuinely understand you or your unique journey hold you back. Often, those quick to criticise are grappling with their own insecurities; their harsh words and opinions serve as a facade, masking deeper vulnerabilities and creating an illusion of self-assuredness. Remember, their judgments say more about them than about you.

35.

Genuine individuals avoid making judgments and instead connect with others through empathy and understanding.

Genuine individuals actively listen and value different perspectives, creating an atmosphere of acceptance and kindness. If you ever find yourself worried about being judged by someone, pause for a moment to consider how authentic that person truly is, as shown by their relationships with others. Authentic people possess a remarkable ability to set aside their judgments and engage with others through empathy and understanding. They consciously strive to listen actively, immersing themselves in the experiences and viewpoints of those around them. By appreciating diverse perspectives, they foster a nurturing environment where everyone feels heard and valued. The next time you feel anxious about potential judgment, reflect on the authenticity of the person in question. Their genuine nature is often revealed through the compassion and openness they show in their relationships with others.

> Just as a judge only accepts evidence in their courtroom, you should only accept thoughts supported by evidence in your mind.
>
> Corinne Coe

36.

Before stressing over what you 'should have done, consider how important it is based on the consequences or impact it will have on you if you don't.

Before you get anxious about what you think you should have accomplished, take a moment to reflect on the true significance of that goal. Consider how it might impact your life if it remains incomplete. This perspective can assist you in prioritising what truly matters on your journey and help you avoid overcommitting yourself. Concentrate on what aligns with your values and will foster your personal growth.

37.

Free yourself from the burden of anxiety that accompanies the pressure to achieve every single goal and aspiration you envision for your life.

Rather than allowing worries to overwhelm you, consider directing your focus toward the specific tasks and responsibilities that require your immediate attention. By prioritising these key activities, you can utilise your energy more efficiently, laying the groundwork for genuine progress and personal development. Embracing this mindset not only helps you manage your time and resources more effectively but also empowers you to take meaningful steps on your journey, one at a time. Embrace the process of honing in on what truly matters, and you might uncover a sense of fulfilment and accomplishment blossoming within you.

38.

Don't focus solely on the one negative incident; instead, emphasise the most positive outcomes.

Instead of fixating on a single negative incident, it's crucial to redirect your attention to the numerous positive outcomes that surpass the negatives. Celebrate the successes and achievements that stemmed from the situation, allowing them to take centre stage in your narrative. Steer clear of solely concentrating on the negative aspects and overlooking the positives. This method not only fosters a more balanced perspective but also promotes a focus on growth and learning.

39.

Consider evaluating yourself based on the feedback from the majority, not just a few. If most people don't see you negatively, then you're likely not as bad as you think.

Take a moment to assess yourself based on the overall feedback you receive from those around you, rather than relying solely on the opinions of a few individuals. If the majority of people in your life hold a positive view or at least do not see you negatively, it's a solid sign that you may be more capable and valuable than you often think. Remember, perceptions can differ greatly, and it's important to understand that the wider consensus can provide a more balanced perspective of who you are.

40.

It's important to keep in mind that feelings aren't facts if you want to arrive at a rational conclusion.

It is crucial to recognise that emotions, while powerful and often overwhelming, do not necessarily reflect reality. When seeking to draw a logical conclusion, distinguishing between our feelings and the actual facts at hand is essential. Emphasising this awareness can help ensure that our judgments are grounded in rationality instead of being swayed by emotional responses.

> If you want to control your emotions, you have to control your thoughts.

Sherry Argov

41.

The next time an event occurs, refrain from exaggerating the negatives or downplaying the positives.

When a new event arises, aim to view it from a balanced perspective. Focus on recognising both the challenges and the positives. By addressing the negative elements without allowing them to dominate your view, you can ensure that the positive contributions are highlighted and appreciated for their importance. This approach fosters more constructive dialogue and encourages a well-rounded understanding of the situation.

42.

People often perceive you differently than you may think.

Our self-image is a complex construct, intricately woven from our beliefs, accomplishments, and emotional responses. It is shaped by our personal experiences and how we interpret our lives. Conversely, when others evaluate us, they do so through the lens of their own biases, experiences, and cultural backgrounds. This can create a significant gap between how we view ourselves and how we are perceived by those around us. Understanding these inherent biases is crucial in bridging the gap between our self-perception and the perceptions held by others. Our internalised view of who we are may not accurately reflect the impression we leave on the world. Therefore, it is important to observe the behaviours and attitudes others show towards us. If you consistently notice positive reactions and behaviours directed your way, it's likely that your worries about how others perceive you are unfounded. Embracing this insight can foster a healthier self-image and a more nuanced understanding of your role in social interactions.

43.

To master the complex skill of emotional regulation, it's essential to take a step back and reflect on instances when your emotional reactions seem overly intense compared to the situation.

Consider moments when minor issues trigger strong emotions, resulting in feelings like frustration, anxiety, or anger. In those crucial instances, take a moment for introspection. Breathe deeply and reflect: "Am I overreacting to this situation?" Assess whether the intensity of your emotional response aligns with the actual stakes involved. Ponder the question, "Is the outcome likely to be as dire as my emotions suggest?" Engage in this thoughtful self-inquiry. Ask yourself, "Is the outcome really as dire as it feels?" This process invites a deeper understanding of your emotional responses. It fosters self-awareness, helping you gain clarity and perspective amidst the chaos of heightened feelings. By regularly practising this reflective approach, you can cultivate a more balanced viewpoint in the face of challenges, turning your reactions into measured responses that enhance emotional well-being.

44.

Remind yourself of your past successes in problem-solving; this should demonstrate your capability, even if you don't feel confident.

Reflect on your past successes in problem-solving, as they can serve as a strong reminder of your capabilities. Can you outline the specific steps you took to tackle a challenge you faced previously? What particular skills and resources did you rely on to find a workable solution? Were you able to resolve the issue independently, or did you seek assistance from your support network? If you were to face a similar issue now, would you feel more at ease, knowing you've developed effective coping strategies, problem-solving techniques, and a reliable support system?

45.

When you find yourself in a situation that triggers anxiety, take deep, slow breaths before and during it. With practice, you'll build confidence in managing anxiety in any scenario.

Whenever you start to feel anxious, take a moment to pause and shift your focus to your breath. Begin by inhaling deeply, holding it for a moment, and then exhaling slowly to help release any built-up tension. This breathing technique can effectively counteract the adrenaline that often contributes to feelings of anxiety. Make it a point to practice deep breathing both before and during anxious moments. Afterwards, take time to acknowledge your efforts and celebrate the progress you've made. With consistent practice, you'll gradually build your confidence and enhance your ability to manage anxiety more effectively.

> Happiness does not depend on what you have or who you are. It solely relies on what you think.
>
> Buddha

46.

Stop overcommitting and stressing about missed deadlines because of a lack of resources and time. If your plate is already full, don't take on more. Focus on your responsibilities and delegate tasks that aren't yours.

When taking on new tasks, assess the time required. If it's substantial, consider delegating a task of equal importance to avoid feeling overwhelmed. The more you take on, the greater your stress and worry will become. Let go of the urge to carry every burden on your own. Focus on the responsibilities that genuinely belong to you and don't hesitate to delegate tasks that fall outside your expertise or time limits. When faced with new assignments, take a moment to evaluate how much time and effort they will demand from you. If the commitment is significant, think about passing off a task of similar weight to maintain balance and prevent feelings of being overwhelmed. Remember, the more you take on without support, the greater your stress and anxiety will grow, making it more difficult to manage your core responsibilities effectively.

47.

When someone asks you for a favour, take a moment to reflect to help avoid overcommitting.

When someone approaches you with a request for a favour, respond by saying, "Leave it with me; I'll get back to you." This phrase not only buys you some valuable time but also gives you the opportunity to pause and contemplate the potential implications of taking on that responsibility. Consider the investment it might require in terms of time, energy, or other commitments you may already have. By taking a moment to reflect on your own capacity, you can make a more informed decision and avoid the pitfalls of overcommitting yourself. This thoughtful approach can foster healthier boundaries and ensure that you only take on what you can truly manage.

48.

You are only accountable for the negative feelings you deliberately cause in others.

It's essential to maintain healthy boundaries when it comes to the struggles of others. While it's natural to want to help those we care about, getting too involved in their issues or trying to fix their emotions can often lead to greater complications. Your role should be one of guidance and support, offering a listening ear or a word of encouragement without taking ownership of their challenges. Each individual faces unique challenges, and it is their responsibility to confront and resolve these issues in their own way. You are accountable for the emotional impact you have on others, particularly if you unintentionally cause discomfort. Therefore, it's important to avoid getting involved in the personal problems of those around you. Instead, focus on empowering them to navigate their own paths. While your insights may be valuable, the journey of self-discovery and resolution ultimately belongs to them. By doing so, you can provide meaningful support without carrying the weight of their burdens.

49.

Don't worry about failing at something new; some things require practice, knowledge, and experience before you can truly master them.

It's completely understandable to feel anxious about the prospect of failing when attempting something new. Remember that many pursuits require commitment, learning, and time to develop the skills necessary for true success. Embrace this journey of practice and growth; understand that mastery often flourishes with patience and perseverance. It's all part of the process, and you're not alone in this experience.

50.

When facing setbacks in the pursuit of a goal, remember that if you demonstrated courage and were willing to step outside your comfort zone, you've only partially failed.

When pursuing a goal and encountering setbacks along the way, it's important to recognise that these moments represent only a small part of failure. Every attempt reflects your bravery and initiative, illustrating your readiness to step beyond the familiar confines of your comfort zone. Engaging in the process reveals your willingness to confront challenges head-on, embrace new experiences, learn valuable lessons, and ultimately cultivate resilience and strength in the face of adversity.

> Your mind leads, your brain fuels, and your body acts. Think positively to trigger your brain's feel-good chemicals
>
> Corinne Coe

51.

You aren't being rejected because you're different or not good enough; you're being rejected because they can't appreciate your courage to be authentic.

It's important to remember that rejection does not reflect your worth or uniqueness. At times, people may find it difficult to acknowledge the courage it takes to be true to oneself. This can be a painful experience, but your authenticity is a true gift. The right people will recognise and appreciate it—so seek out your community.

52.

You shouldn't worry about the opinions of those who lack the substance or credibility to offer meaningful judgment.

It's unnecessary to be swayed by the opinions of individuals who lack the depth or credibility to provide insightful or meaningful judgments. Their perspectives often stem from ignorance or superficiality, and engaging with such viewpoints can divert you from more valuable feedback. Instead, prioritise insights from people whose experiences and knowledge genuinely enrich the conversation.

53.

If there's a strong chance that the worst-case scenario might happen, it's essential to assess the potential impact it could have on you.

When confronted with the possibility of a worst-case scenario, it's crucial to assess carefully the potential consequences it could have on your life. Take the time to consider how deeply it might impact you—your emotions, your relationships, and your overall well-being. If, after reflecting, you decide that the effects would be minimal or manageable, it's wise to let go of any worries surrounding the situation, even if the event may still occur. Understanding the actual stakes can help you prioritise your concerns and focus on what truly matters.

54.

When facing change, consider whether your fear arises from believing you can't adapt or from the change itself.

Take a moment to reflect on the changes you've experienced in the past. Did you find yourself afraid of your own ability to adapt, or was it the change itself that caused fear? The truth is, you had the skills and resilience needed to navigate those shifts; often, it was your own wavering confidence that fueled your anxiety. The next time you feel that familiar sense of unease creeping in, take a deep breath and remind yourself of the strengths you carry within. Recognise your capacity to face challenges head-on and trust in your resources to guide you through.

55.

Stop trying to create a fail-safe plan for your future by gathering too much information.

Rather than getting caught up in the endless pursuit of a perfect plan for your future by collecting an overwhelming amount of information, take a moment to reflect on past experiences when you felt unprepared. Recall those times when uncertainty loomed, yet you found a way through. You relied on your innate skills and the knowledge you had acquired, allowing your adaptability to shine in challenging situations. Trust in your ability to navigate obstacles as they arise, knowing that you have the resilience to find solutions in the face of the unknown. Embrace the journey ahead with confidence in your capacity to adjust and thrive.

Corinne Coe is a practising psychologist in Australia with over 20 years of experience treating individuals with depression, anxiety, and other mental health issues. Her areas of interest include personal development and relationships. She is a blogger and public speaker, facilitates workshops, and is the author of two other self-help books, "Heal Your Mind, Heal Your Life" and "From Passive to Assertive".

www.corinnecoe.com

www.ingramcontent.com/pod-product-compliance
Lightning Source LLC
Chambersburg PA
CBHW061157010526
44119CB00059B/850